T0127719

Endorsements

"Wow! What an encouraging and inspiring book. It's not a book to just read once, but to daily take sections and pray, reflect, and muse over each word that points to God the Father, the Son and the Holy Spirit. It's worth the time to have a deeper walk and grow in your journey, this side of heaven, by using these writings."

- BERNIE ELLIOT
  National Bible Quiz Coordinator, Assemblies of God

"Mercy Dworzak is a brilliant mind and a shining spirit. This follow-on to Simple Praise continues that tradition of using the Word of God to create the thoughts and set the tone for a healthy devotional life. Mercy's ability to distill the essence really helps focus the heart on what is most important. The title may say "simple", but the content is profound."

- DR. JOSEPH B. FUITEN
  Pastor Emeritus, Cedar Park Assembly of God

Revolutionize Your Prayer Life and Overcome Anxieties

SIMPLE PRAYER

Help for a new believer in Jesus

MERCY DWORZAK

WESTBOW
PRESS®
A DIVISION OF THOMAS NELSON
& ZONDERVAN

Copyright © 2018 Mercy Dworzak.

All rights reserved. No part of this book may be used or reproduced by any means, graphic, electronic, or mechanical, including photocopying, recording, taping or by any information storage retrieval system without the written permission of the author except in the case of brief quotations embodied in critical articles and reviews.

WestBow Press books may be ordered through booksellers or by contacting:

WestBow Press
A Division of Thomas Nelson & Zondervan
1663 Liberty Drive
Bloomington, IN 47403
www.westbowpress.com
1 (866) 928-1240

Because of the dynamic nature of the Internet, any web addresses or links contained in this book may have changed since publication and may no longer be valid. The views expressed in this work are solely those of the author and do not necessarily reflect the views of the publisher, and the publisher hereby disclaims any responsibility for them.

Any people depicted in stock imagery provided by Getty Images are models, and such images are being used for illustrative purposes only. Certain stock imagery © Getty Images.

All Scripture quotations, unless otherwise indicated, are taken from the Holy Bible, New International Version®, NIV®. Copyright ©1973, 1978, 1984, 2011 by Biblica, Inc.™ Used by permission of Zondervan. All rights reserved worldwide. www.zondervan.com The "NIV" and "New International Version" are trademarks registered in the United States Patent and Trademark Office by Biblica, Inc.™

Scripture taken from the New King James Version®. Copyright © 1982 by Thomas Nelson. Used by permission. All rights reserved.

Scripture quotations marked (TLB) are taken from The Living Bible copyright © 1971. Used by permission of Tyndale House Publishers, Inc., Carol Stream, Illinois 60188. All rights reserved.

ISBN: 978-1-9736-3464-5 (sc)
ISBN: 978-1-9736-3463-8 (e)

Print information available on the last page.

WestBow Press rev. date: 09/10/2018

Dedication

To my family that loves the Lord Jesus Christ

and are devoted to serving Him.

Contents

Introduction

Worshiping God, reading his word, and talking to him daily are essential elements to growing as children of God. By doing so we get to know God, to love God, and to serve God.

Our heavenly Father is the giver of good gifts. He loads us with benefits more than we can ask or imagine. He desires his children to seek his face and request his help. He wants to answer our prayers.

Jesus said in Matthew 7:7,

"Ask and it will be given to you;
seek and you will find;
knock and the door will be opened to you".

His answer may not be exactly what we asked for, but will certainly bring the best outcome in our lives.

In this world, we have troubles and anxieties, but Paul has showed us how to overcome anxieties and live a victorious life.

In Philippians 4:6-7 Paul says,

> *"Do not be anxious about anything, but in every situation, by prayer and petition, with thanksgiving, present your requests to God. And the peace of God, which transcends all understanding, will guard your hearts and your minds in Christ Jesus."*

When we invite God into our troubles, sicknesses, and struggles, we can be relieved of our anxieties, **while God is working out our solution.**

Paul exhorts us to present our requests with thanksgiving.

Thanksgiving is an expression of our faith in God. Faith honors God. God is FAITHFUL to honor our faith. When we praise and thank God, we acknowledge that God exists and that He is the source of all the good things we have come to possess and accomplish. We praise God for WHO HE IS and thank God for WHAT HE DOES. **Being grateful helps us more than anything else because gratitude renews our mind and brings healing to our soul and body.**

Praising God prospers our soul. We cannot give God anything without receiving manifold blessings in return. It is not that we "have to" give God praise but WHO GOD IS warrants our praise and worship. We can praise God alone or in a congregation of believers. Both are necessary!

Worship is more than praise and thanksgiving. Our entire life is worship – what we do with our life and how we do it demonstrates what and whom we worship. **We live out, with all our strength, what we really believe and love with all our heart, soul and mind**. That is why Jesus said in Matthew 22:37, *"Love the Lord your God with all your heart, with all your soul and with all your mind."* This is worship!

God has given us everything we need for life here on earth and in eternity. Jesus has redeemed us, sanctified us, and qualified us for an everlasting fellowship with God the Father. Let us thank God for His amazing grace, and for the good and perfect gifts He bestows on us daily.

When our petitions are presented with praise and thanksgiving,

> our heart will be changed,
> our mind will be renewed,

our spirit will be strengthened,
and our soul will prosper.
We are not only healed but made whole.

Let us therefore boldly enter the courts of our God, with praise and thanksgiving, and present our requests with confidence to our most gracious Father.

Our Father in heaven hallowed be your name

Matthew 6:9b

SECTION 1

PRAISE

Praise the Father

Father Loves

God is the Creator of the heavens and the earth, the author of all life, and has no beginning or end.

This all-knowing God knew, before He created man, that He must sacrifice Jesus His Son to purchase man back from the kingdom of darkness that would enslave. He knew that He must send the Holy Spirit to guide man through his earthly journey, and to lead man to his eternal home. Despite the cost of the sacrifice required to redeem man, God said, "Let us make man" Genesis 1:26. This is the Father heart of God!

Love Gives!

Father God longs for his children to come home to him.

No matter how young or old you are, you have a Father in heaven. He is the Ancient of Days. He is watching over you every moment of the day, caring for all your needs, and waiting for you to run into his arms for strength and comfort.

In the next few pages you can read about and praise this awesome God, our Father.

Father I Honor You

God, the blessed and only Ruler, the King of Kings and Lord of Lords, who alone is immortal and who lives in unapproachable light, whom no one has seen or can see. To him be honor and might forever. Amen.

1 Timothy 6:15b – 16

Father you are God Most High.

Father you are Creator of everything.

Father you are Majesty in Heaven.

Father you are King of all the earth.

Father you have no beginning or end of life.

Father you are God of Divine nature.

Father you are Almighty.

Father you are Holy and True.

Father you are Eternal.

Father you are Ancient of Days.

Father you are the Majestic Glory.

Father you are the God of Peace.

Father you are the Everlasting One.

Father you are Kind.

Father you are Tolerant.

Father you are Longsuffering.

Father you are full of Compassion.

Father you are Merciful.

Father you are Forgiving.

Father you are Patient.

Father you are Slow to Anger.

Father you are Faithful.

Father you are Just.

Father you are Love.

Father you are Gracious.

Father you are consuming Fire.

Father you are the Mighty Warrior.

Father you are Invincible.

Father you are Great, and your Hand is strong.

Father you are Mighty and firm in your Purpose.

Father you are the God of Order.

Father you are the God of our spirit.

Father you are Greater than any mortal.

Father you do not let mortals prevail against you.

Father you are not a human being to change your mind.

Father you are not human, so you don't lie.

Father you are not slow in keeping your promises.

Father you are the Light and in you there is no evil at all.

Father you are the Righteous Judge.

Father you are the zealous God.

Father you are the Builder of everything.

Father you are Strong.

Father you are a Rock of Refuge.

Father you are a mighty Fortress.

Father you are the God of glorious riches.

Father your word is Right and True.

Father your voice is majestic.

Father your voice is like the sound of rushing water.

Father I Worship You

"Great and marvelous are your deeds, Lord God Almighty.

Just and true are your ways, King of the nations.

Who will not fear you, Lord, and bring glory to your name?

For you alone are holy. All nations will come and worship before you, for your righteous acts have been revealed."

Revelation 15:3b-4

Father your voice is powerful.

Father your voice shakes the desert.

Father your voice twists the oaks and strips the forests bare.

Father your voice strikes with flashes of lightning.

Father you are greatly to be feared.

Father your works are Awesome and Mighty.

Father you are the King of Heaven.

Father you are God in heaven above and on the earth below.

Father you are God of invisible qualities.

Father you are Spirit.

Father you are OMNIPOTENT.

Father you are OMNIPRESENT.

Father you are OMNICIENT.

Father you are exalted in your Power.

Father you are worthy of all Glory.

Father you are Sovereign over all the kingdoms on the earth.

Father You Alone Are God

LORD Almighty, the God of Israel, enthroned between the cherubim, you alone are God over all the kingdoms of the earth. You made the heaven and earth.

Isaiah 37:16

Father you are Immutable.

Father you live in unapproachable light.

Father your Name is Holy.

Father your Name is Great and Awesome.

Father your Name is Jehovah Jireh – our Provider.

Father your Name is Jehovah Shalom – our Peace.

Father your Name is Jehovah Rapha – our Healer.

Father your Name is Jehovah Sabaoth – Lord of Hosts.

Father you are seated on your holy throne.

Father you are enthroned between the cherubim.

Father you are clothed with splendor and majesty.

Father you are forever praised and adored.

Father your kingdom is an eternal kingdom.

Father you are King of the nations.

Father your dominion endures throughout all generations.

Father There Is None Like You

Who is like you, LORD God Almighty? You, LORD, are mighty, and your faithfulness surrounds you.

Psalm 89:8

Father you are enthroned as the Holy One.

Father your years will never end.

Father you are AMAZING.

Father you are AWESOME.

Father you are WONDERFUL.

Father you are MARVELOUS.

Father you are The GREAT I AM.

Prayer Notes

Praise Jesus the Son

Jesus Saves

God made man in his image and had constant fellowship with him in the garden of Eden. But when man sinned by disobeying God, man's spirit died and he was separated from God. As there is no way man can earn forgiveness for his sins by any works he can do on this earth, God, who is Holy and Righteous, himself made a way.

At the appointed time, God the Father sent his word to become flesh. The only begotten Son of God, Jesus, became the Son of man. God who is holy, cannot let sin go unpunished. Therefore, he placed the sins of all mankind, past, present and future, upon Jesus as he hung on the cross. Through Jesus Christ, God reconciled all men to himself.

Jesus came into the world to save us sinners and to restore our relationship to our Father. Jesus chose to endure the ridicule and the cruel death at the hands of men rather than to live without mankind for all eternity.

Jesus is our Savior, Redeemer, Friend and much more. In the next few pages you will be blessed to learn all that he is, and can be, in your life.

Jesus I Give You Glory

Worthy is the Lamb, who was slain, to receive power and wealth, and wisdom and strength and honor and glory and praise!

Revelation 5:12b

Jesus you are the Son of God Most High.

Jesus you are God who WAS and IS and who IS to Come.

Jesus you are the Bright and Morning Star.

Jesus you are the Faithful and the True Witness from God.

Jesus you are the Ruler of all Creation.

Jesus you are the Image of the Invisible God.

Jesus you are the exact Representation of God the Father.

Jesus you are the Firstborn over all Creation.

Jesus you are the Heir of all things.

Jesus you are the Sustainer who holds all things together.

Jesus you are far Above all rule and authority.

Jesus you are Seated at the right hand of the Father in Heaven.

Jesus you have Sovereignty over everything.

Jesus you are the Treasure House of Wisdom.

Jesus you are the Source of all Knowledge.

Jesus you are the Word that created all things.

Jesus you are Head over all power.

Jesus your Name is far Above every name.

Jesus your Wisdom is great and awesome.

Jesus your Purposes are eternal.

Jesus your Dominion is an everlasting dominion.

Jesus you Rule over the nations.

Jesus you are the Righteous One.

Jesus you are the Great God.

Jesus you are the WORD of God.

Jesus you are the WORD of Life.

Jesus you are the King of the Ages.

Jesus you are the Only Begotten Son of God.

Jesus you are the Seed of the Woman.

Jesus you are the Wisdom of God.

Jesus you are the Lord of the Sabbath.

Jesus you are the Lion of Judah.

Jesus you are the Great High Priest forever.

Jesus you are the Chief Cornerstone.

Jesus you are the Faithful Scribe.

Jesus you are the Stone the builders rejected.

Jesus you are the Root of Jesse.

Jesus you are the Son of David.

Jesus you are the Messiah.

Jesus you are the Christ.

Jesus you are the Anointed One.

Jesus you are LORD.

Jesus you are Gracious.

Jesus you are Humble.

Jesus you are Good.

Jesus you are the Redeemer.

Jesus you are the Beloved Son of God.

Jesus you are the Author of Salvation.

Jesus I Give You Praise

To him who sits on the throne and to the Lamb be praise and honor and glory and power, for ever and ever!"

Revelation 5:13b

Jesus you are the Word made Flesh.

Jesus you are the Lamb Without Blemish.

Jesus you are the Passover Lamb.

Jesus you are the Power of God for Salvation.

Jesus you are the Bread of Life from Heaven.

Jesus you are the Atoning sacrifice.

Jesus you are the Fragrant Offering to God.

Jesus you are Holy, Blameless and Pure.

Jesus you are Mighty to Save.

Jesus you are the Savior of the world.

Jesus you are the Risen Lord.

Jesus you are Alive Forevermore.

Jesus your Love surpasses all knowledge.

Jesus your Blood speaks forgiveness.

Jesus your Gospel is the Word of Truth.

Jesus you are the Light of the world.

Jesus you are the Spring of Living Water.

Jesus you are much Superior to the Angels.

Jesus you are Head over all things of the church.

Jesus you are Glorified through the church.

Jesus you are the Builder of broken lives.

Jesus you are the Bearer of our burdens.

Jesus you are the Deliverer.

Jesus you are the Door.

Jesus you are the Way.

Jesus you are the Truth.

Jesus you are the Life.

Jesus you are the Justifier.

Jesus you are the Last Adam.

Jesus you are the Intercessor.

Jesus you are the Rebuilder of broken walls.

Jesus you are the Restorer of the lost.

Jesus you are the Mediator of the New Covenant.

Jesus you are the Captain of Our Salvation.

Jesus you are the Great Advocate between God and Man.

Jesus you are the Chief Shepherd.

Jesus you are the Great Physician.

Jesus you are the Same yesterday, today and forever.

Jesus you are the Ture Vine.

Jesus you are the Author and Finisher of our faith.

Jesus you are the Author of Life.

Jesus you are the Baptizer in the Holy Spirit.

Jesus you are the Everlasting Father.

Jesus you are the Prince of Peace.

Jesus you are the Wonderful Counselor.

Jesus you are the Mighty God.

Jesus you are the Living One.

Jesus you are the Manna from Heaven.

Jesus you are the Living Stone.

Jesus you are the Mighty Tower.

Jesus you are the Precious Cornerstone

Jesus you are the Prophet of the Lord.

Jesus you are the Rock of Salvation.

Jesus you are the Mighty Warrior of God.

Jesus you are the Protector.

Jesus you are the Stronghold in trouble.

Jesus you are the Judge and the Lawgiver.

Jesus you are the Gift from heaven beyond description.

Jesus you are the Firstborn from the Dead.

Jesus you are the Resurrection and the Life.

Jesus you are the Dayspring from on High.

Jesus you are the Friend.

Jesus you are the Kinsman Redeemer.

Jesus you are the Faithful Lover.

Jesus you are the Heavenly Bridegroom.

Jesus you are the Fairest of ten thousand.

Jesus you are the Rose of Sharon.

Jesus you are the Lily of the Valley.

Jesus you are All together lovely.

Jesus you are my Song.

Jesus you are the Lover of my soul.

Jesus you are the Hope of Glory.

Jesus you are the Victorious one.

Jesus you are God who Ascended to Heaven.

Jesus you are worshipped by all God's angels.

Jesus you are Exalted to the Highest place.

Jesus you are Crowned with glory and honor.

Jesus you are the Alpha and Omega.

Jesus you are the Beginning and the End.

Jesus you are the First and the Last.

Jesus I Adore You

Now to the King eternal, immortal, invisible, the only God, be honor and glory for ever and ever. Amen

1 Timothy 1:17

Jesus you are the God "I Am".

Jesus you are the soon and coming King.

Jesus you are the Lord of Glory.

Jesus you are the King of Kings.

Jesus you are GOD.

Prayer Notes

Praise the Holy Spirit

Holy Spirit Helps

Holy Spirit is Jesus in us. When Jesus was on the earth, his presence was limited by location. Jesus said that it would be beneficial for us that He would leave the earth and ascend to heaven. Because then the Father would send the Holy Spirit to come and dwell inside of us.

Jesus had to shed his blood for the cleansing of our sins, so the Holy Spirit can come and live inside of us. Before Jesus, the blood of goats and bulls sacrificed, as sin offerings, could only cover the sins of the people. But the blood of Jesus removes our sins and makes us clean so we can receive the gift of the Holy Spirit.

God the Father pours out his Spirit on those who ask him. So, ask and you will receive.

In the next few pages you can come to know and praise the Holy Spirit who is our helper and much more.

Holy Spirit
Live In Me

And I will ask the Father, and he will give you another advocate to help and be with you forever – the Spirit of truth. The world cannot accept him, because it neither sees him nor knows him. But you know him, for he lives with you and will be in you.

John 14:16-17

Holy Spirit you are the Comforter.

Holy Spirit you are the Helper.

Holy Spirit you are the Guide.

Holy Spirit you are the Teacher.

Holy Spirit you are the Counselor.

Holy Spirit you are the Advocate.

Holy Spirit you are the unsurpassed Wisdom of God.

Holy Spirit you are the unfailing Love of God.

Holy Spirit you are the incomparable Power of God.

Holy Spirit you are the Seal of ownership.

Holy Spirit you are the Guarantee of the heavenly inheritance.

Holy Spirit you are the Foretaste of future glory.

Holy Spirit you are the Presence and the Power of God in us.

Holy Spirit you know the Mind of God.

Holy Spirit you bring Revelation from heaven.

Holy Spirit you give us God's Life.

Holy Spirit Work In Me

But the Advocate, the Holy Spirit, whom the Father will send in my name, will teach you all things and will remind you of everything I have said to you.

John 14:26

Holy Spirit you bring us God's Mercy.

Holy Spirit you are the Spirit of Truth.

Holy Spirit you remind God's truth to us.

Holy Spirit you sanctify us.

Holy Spirit you destroy the yoke of burden.

Holy Spirit you help us overcome sinful cravings.

Holy Spirit you break the chains of bondage.

Holy Spirit you help us worship God.

Holy Spirit you pray through us.

Holy Spirit you speak through us.

Holy Spirit you enlighten our minds.

Holy Spirit you renew our minds.

Holy Spirit you lead us into all truth.

Holy Spirit you live inside of us.

Holy Spirit you fill us with joy.

Holy Spirit you fill us with love.

Holy Spirit Live Through Me

God has raised this Jesus to Life, and we are all witnesses of it. Exalted to the right hand of God, he has received from the Father the promised Holy Spirit and has poured out what you now see and hear.

Acts 2:32-33

Holy Spirit you give strength and power to our inner man.

Holy Spirit you fill us with confident hope.

Holy Spirit you give us holy boldness.

Holy Spirit you give us the power to be a witness.

Holy Spirit you bring to remembrance the words of Jesus.

Holy Spirit you instruct us the way God has chosen for us.

Holy Spirit you empower us to stand strong in faith.

Holy Spirit you are the Gift of God to us.

Jesus You Are My Savior

Thank You For Saving Me

Your Sacrifice Is Sufficient

We all, like sheep, have gone astray, each of us has turned to our own way; and the LORD has laid on him the iniquity of us all. He was oppressed and afflicted, yet he did not open his mouth; he was led like a lamb to the slaughter, and as sheep before its shearers is silent, so he did not open his mouth.

Isaiah 53:6-7

How much more, then, will the blood of Christ, who through the eternal Spirit offered himself unblemished to God, cleanse our conscience from acts that lead to death, so that we may serve the living God!

Hebrews 9:14

Father, you so loved the whole world you sent Jesus.

You did not send Jesus to condemn the world.

You did not send Jesus to judge the world.

You sent Jesus to seek and save the lost.

Jesus, you came into the world to save sinners.

You came to rescue the perishing.

You humbled yourself and became a man.

You were not ashamed to be called my God.

You chose me before the creation of the world.

You died so I can have eternal life.

You died for me while I was still a sinner.

You died as a ransom to set me free.

You tasted death on my behalf.

You destroyed the power of death over me.

You rescued me from the kingdom of darkness.

You saved me from the hand of the enemy who wants to destroy me.

Your Salvation
Is A Gift

For the wages of sin is death, but the gift of
God is eternal life in Christ Jesus our Lord.

Romans 6:23

But the gift is not like the trespass. For if
the many died by the trespass of the one
man, how much more did God's grace and
the gift that came by the grace of the one
man, Jesus Christ, overflow to the many!

Romans 5:15

You did not count my sins against me.

You bore my sins in your body on the tree.

You nailed to the cross everything that condemned me.

You offered yourself as a sacrifice to God.

You provided purification for my sins.

Your precious blood justified me.

You redeemed me from being a slave to sin.

You forgave all my sins.

You rescued me from judgment and hell fire.

You brought me into your eternal kingdom.

You reconciled me with my Heavenly Father.

You made me a new creation.

You made me a child of God.

You lavished on me the gift of righteousness.

You gave me access to the holy presence of God.

You saved me not because of what I have done.

Your Grace Is Amazing

Like the rest, we were by nature deserving of wrath. But because of his great love for us, God, who is rich in mercy, made us alive with Christ even when we were dead in transgressions – it is by grace you have been saved.

Ephesians 2:3b-5

You saved me because of your mercy and love.

Your obedience has made me righteous.

Your resurrection has given me hope.

You are the door to the Father in heaven.

Your salvation is for me and my household.

You are the WAY, the TRUTH, and the LIFE.

Jesus there is no other name but your name that saves.

You are my SAVIOR!

Your kingdom come your will be done on earth as it is in heaven

Matthew 6:10

SECTION 2

PURPOSE

The Kingdom Of God Is In Me

I Seek Your Purpose

You Are
My Creator

Your eyes saw my unformed body; all the days ordained for me were written in your book before one of them came to be.

Psalm 139:16

Jesus takes His place on the throne of our hearts when we receive him as our Lord and Savior.

Our Creator has meticulously planned how and for what purpose he brings us to this earth. He selected our parents, the place and time of our birth, the color of our hair, and every detail about us, so we can fulfill his divine purpose.

Not only does God have a unique purpose – what we ought to fulfill in our lives, but also a wonderful plan of how we can fulfill that divine purpose. He created us in our mother's womb and knows what is best for us. He reveals his plans to us through the Holy Spirit. The Holy Spirit guides us and empowers us to do God's will on a daily basis.

When we seek the help of the Holy Spirit and do His will every day we are following His plan and fulfilling His purpose. Thus, God reigns in our lives and extends His kingdom through us.

Paul writes in 2 Corinthians 2:14b,

> *"and uses us to spread the*
> *aroma of the knowledge of him everywhere".*

It does not matter what our vocation. God has good works for us to do in every situation. God wants to manifest his love, his goodness, and his wisdom through his children. God can be glorified through our lives in all places, at all times, and in all seasons.

When we live by the Master's plan, we will have purpose, love, joy, and peace that the world cannot give or take away.

Your Plan Is Prosperous

For you created my inmost being; you knit me together in my mother's womb. I praise you because I am fearfully and wonderfully made; your works are wonderful, I know that full well.

Psalm 139:13-14

For I know the plans I have for you, "declares the LORD, "plans to prosper you and not to harm you, plans to give you hope and a future.

Jeremiah 29:11

You formed man out of the dust of the earth.

You breathed into man your breath of life.

You formed me in my mother's womb.

You have set me apart from birth.

You created me for your purpose.

You have called me by name.

You have a marvelous plan for my life.

Your plan for my life is to prosper me.

Your plan for my life gives me a future.

Your plan for my life gives me hope.

You know when I sit down and when I arise.

You know my thoughts before I speak them out.

You have determined the days of my existence on earth.

You are with me if I go to the deepest depth a man can reach.

You are with me if I go to the highest height a man can reach.

You see me always whether I am in the light or in the dark.

Your Thoughts
Are Immense

How precious to me are your thoughts, God!

How vast is the sum of them!

Psalm 139:17

Your thoughts over me are more than the number of the sand.

Your thoughts over me are precious to me.

Father reveal the mystery of your purpose to me.

Equip me to fulfill your purpose.

Open doors for me that no one can shut.

Help me gain knowledge and understanding.

Give me insight and intelligence.

Give me wisdom and tact of speech.

Fill my future with new opportunities.

Bring to focus the vision for my future.

Bestow abundant provision of grace on me.

Keep my lamp burning for your glory.

Give me the ability to make right decisions.

Help me know the hope of your calling in my life.

Enlighten my mind by your Spirit.

Help me fulfill the purpose you have for me.

Your Purpose
Is Firm

I am the LORD your God, who teaches you
what is best for you, who directs you in the
way you should go.

Isaiah 48:17b

You know what is going to happen in the future.

Sharpen my vision like that of an eagle.

You are the author and finisher of my faith.

You hold the seasons of my life in your precious hands.

You will not allow the evil one to destroy my destiny.

You are faithful to complete the good work you started in me.

You are my POTTER – I am the clay.

Let Your Light Shine Through Me

I Seek Your Will

Jesus
Be Glorified

"For we are God's handiwork, created in Christ Jesus to do good works, which God prepared in advance for us to do."

Ephesians 2:10.

God's will for our lives is for us to know Him and to make Him known.

The scripture says God has pre-determined the good works that we must do as his beloved children.

God has made it possible for us to do those good works through the Holy Spirit that dwells in us. **Our mission is to live out God's love, grace, and truth, wherever we are and in whatever we do.** Then our heavenly Father is honored and glorified. Jesus tells us in Matthew 5:16,

In the same way, let your light shine before others, that they may see your good deeds and glorify your Father in heaven.

Nothing on earth – neither devil, nor sickness, nor defeat – can hinder our destiny when we are fully engaged in following the direction of the Holy Spirit and doing God's will in our lives. Jesus has purchased healing for our body, soul, and mind. He will deliver us from the evil one and guide us on our journey.

Abundant life – a life full of joy, peace, and purpose – is not relative to the earthly things we possess or to the power to acquire them. It is what God enables us to experience as we do His will and fulfill His purpose.

Let us be steadfast in seeking God's help to shine His goodness, His righteousness, and His love to the world around us.

Your Holy Spirit Counsels Me

But the Advocate, the Holy Spirit, whom the Father will send in my name, will teach you all things and will remind you of everything I have said to you.

John 14:26

Who is wise and understanding among you? Let them show it by their good life, by deeds done in the humility that comes from wisdom.

James 3:13

Father pour out your Spirit upon me.

Jesus baptize me with the Holy Spirit.

Holy Spirit help me worship God in truth.

Holy Spirit I do not want to stifle you.

Holy Spirit I do not want to grieve you.

Father fill me the gifts of the Holy Spirit.

Father empower me by your Spirit of Power.

Reveal the depth of your love and grace to me.

Reveal the mystery of the Gospel to me.

Enable me to do good deeds.

Fill me with wisdom that is pure.

Fill me with wisdom that is considerate.

Fill me with wisdom that is peace-loving.

Fill me with wisdom that is impartial and sincere.

Fill me with wisdom that is full of mercy.

Empower me for works done by faith.

Your Holy Spirit Strengthens Me

Let us not become weary in doing good, for at the proper time we will reap a harvest if we do not give up.

Galatians 6:9

For God did not give us a spirit of timidity, but a spirit of power, of love and of self-discipline.

2 Timothy 1:7

Fill my heart with love for people around me.

Help me to be known as a friendly person.

Help me to be known as a loving person.

Help me be your touch of kindness to others.

Guard my mind with peace.

Give me a sober spirit.

Give me discernment.

Give me sound judgement.

Help me think clearly and make good choices.

Give me strength to overcome troubles.

Fill me with confident hope.

Increase my faith.

Help me be steadfast in prayer.

Help me be rooted and grounded in love.

Train my hands for works that will defeat the enemy.

Ignite my heart with a passion for the lost around me.

Help Me
Serve You

And God is able to bless you abundantly,
so that in all things at all times, having
all that you need, you will abound in every
good work.

2 Corinthians 9:8

To him who loves us and has freed us from
our sins by his blood, and has made us to be
a kingdom and priests to serve his God and
Father – to him be glory and power for ever
and ever! Amen.

Revelation 1:5b-6

Reveal your purpose for me in this place.

Help me represent Jesus in a relevant way.

Help me see what you see in others.

Help me bring healing and comfort to others.

Help me bring joy to the heart of others.

Help me serve you whole-heartedly.

Enable me to speak your word with boldness.

Holy Spirit remind me of the words of Jesus.

Holy Spirit speak through me.

Let your presence go with me.

Let your word in my heart flow like living water.

Let my words enrich peoples' lives around me.

Surround me with your favor and shield me.

Work in me to do all that is pleasing to you.

I want to do YOUR WILL!

Give us today our daily bread

Matthew 6:11

SECTION 3

PETITION

Everlasting Father Is My Provider.

I Seek Your Provision

Your Provision
Is Plentiful

Therefore, I tell you, do not worry about your life, what you will eat or drink; or about your body, what you will wear... Look at the birds of the air; they do not sow or reap or store away in barns, and yet your heavenly Father, feeds them. Are you not much more valuable than they?

But seek first his kingdom and his righteousness, and all these things will be given to you as well.

Matthew 6:25-26, 33

Father, you provide for the just and unjust.

You provide abundantly.

You send rain to the earth.

You provide grass for the cattle.

You care for birds of the air.

You tell me I am valuable.

You provide for all my needs.

You load me with benefits every day.

You give me every good and perfect gift.

You sustain me by your power.

You care about all my problems.

You help me in my time of need.

You listen to all my prayers.

You answer me from your holy throne.

You use the wrong anyone does to me for good.

You do what is just and right for me.

Your Resource Is Unlimited

And my God will meet all your needs according to the riches of his glory in Christ Jesus.

Philippians 4:19

The LORD is my shepherd, I lack nothing. He makes me lie down in green pastures, he leads me beside quiet water, he refreshes my soul.

Psalm 23:1-2

Father you lift me when I fall.

Help me through this difficulty.

Help me for I am powerless.

Spare me from sorrow.

Help me not be overwhelmed by worldly worries.

Make a way in the wilderness for me.

Make streams to flow in the desert for me.

You do what is impossible for me to do.

Remove my grieving clothes and clothe me with joy.

Give me the ability to tackle everything that comes my way.

Turn my problems into opportunities.

Make me stand in confidence and strength.

Help me make the best of everything I have.

You are my Shepherd taking care of all my needs.

You are with me wherever I go.

You deal bountifully with me.

Your Supply Is Bountiful

He has shown kindness by giving you rain from heaven and crops in their seasons; he provides you with plenty of food and fills your heart with joy.

Acts 14:17b

He grants peace to your borders and satisfies you with the finest of wheat.

Psalm 147:14

You reward me for working diligently.

You give me riches and restore my fortune.

You give me power to enjoy wealth.

Help me be successful at work.

Help me accomplish the task set before me.

Help me to be focused and disciplined.

Prosper the work of my hands.

Help me stand strong in faith.

Take care of all my tomorrows.

Fill my heart with joy that nothing can take away.

Give me peace when I lie down to rest.

Strengthen my heart.

Turn your face towards me.

Be gracious to me.

You are my rising sun.

You make my face radiant.

Your Faithfulness Is Everlasting

For I have always been mindful of your unfailing love and have lived in reliance on your faithfulness.

Psalm 26:3

Your love, LORD, reaches to the heavens, your faithfulness to the skies.

Psalm 36:5

You give me a happy heart.

You call me beautiful.

Your love for me is unfailing.

You are forever faithful.

You are my PROVIDER!

I Seek Your Help

God is our Father no matter in what circumstance we find ourselves today. He is the defender of the fatherless and the widow. He takes care of the orphan, the poor, and the needy. Jesus says in Matthew 10:29 that even a tiny sparrow does not fall to the ground without the Father's care.

Our Father is a shelter from the storm, a stronghold in the time of trouble, and a refuge from the attack of the evil one. He is faithful to us even when we are not faithful to Him.

He hears our cry for help and comes to our rescue quickly. He answers all our prayers according to His will. He formed us in our mother's womb and knows what is best for us. He calls us by name and loves us unconditionally.

He does not give us according to what our deeds deserve because He is merciful, but loads us with benefits that we do not deserve because He is gracious. He is committed to helping us to our very end. There is no one like our God.

He is our loving FATHER!

Your Help Is Ever Present

God is our refuge and strength, an ever-present help in trouble.

Psalm 46:1

My help comes from the LORD, the Maker of heaven and earth. He will not let your foot slip – he who watches over you will not slumber;

Psalm 121:2-3

You defend the fatherless.

You rescue the lost.

You restore the broken.

You heal the wounded.

You embrace the rejected.

You lift the cast down.

You help the helpless.

You strengthen the weak.

You support the needy.

You provide for the poor.

You give hope to the forsaken.

You are the redeemer of the deserted.

You are the caretaker of the abandoned.

You are the lover of my soul.

Consider the yearning in my heart.

Satisfy me with the joy of your presence.

Your Help
Is Abundant

There is no one like ... God ... who rides across the heavens to help you and on the clouds in his majesty.

Deuteronomy 33:26

The LORD is my strength and my shield; my heart trusts in him, and he helps me. My heart leaps for joy, and with my song I praise him.

Psalm 28:7

Open my ears to hear what the Holy Spirit is saying to me.

Open my eyes to see what the Holy Spirit is showing me.

I fix my eyes on you.

I will not be afraid.

I hold on to your promises.

I humble my soul with fasting.

I cast all my cares on you.

I am the work of your hand.

I belong to you.

You have not forsaken me and you never will.

Rejoicing in you gives me strength.

Rejoicing in you lights up my face.

You are my ever-present help.

You are my HELPER!

Jesus By
Your Stripes
I am Healed

I Seek Your Healing

Your Healing Is Precious

"He himself bore our sins" in his body on the cross, so that we might die to sins and live for righteousness; "by his wounds you have been healed."

1 Peter 2:24

Jesus, you are the Miracle Worker!

You fed the five thousand with five loaves of bread.

You walked on the water and brought the storm to calm.

You opened blind eyes with a touch of your hand.

You made the deaf to hear and the mute to speak.

You cleansed the leper and caused the lame to walk.

You raised the widow's son, and Lazarus from the dead.

Your cured the incurable and made them whole.

You healed all who were under the power of the devil.

Jesus by your stripes you have purchased my healing for today.

Your body was broken to make my body whole.

You took all my weaknesses and bore all my sicknesses.

Your gracious Word brings healing to my bones.

Your precious blood cleanses my body.

Fill me with strength as I wait on you.

Hold me up with your righteous right hand.

Your Healing
Is Priceless

LORD God Almighty says in Exodus 15:26b

"I am the LORD, who heals you."

Worship the LORD your God, and his blessing will be on your food and water. I will take away sickness from among you.

Exodus 23:25

Bring health and wholeness to my mind.

Renew my mind by your Spirit.

Give me a keen and sound mind.

Refresh my soul by your Spirit.

Heal my wounds and strengthen my heart.

Fill me with power for I am tired and worn out.

Rescue my body from wasting away in grief.

Rescue me from the grave so I can fulfill your purpose.

Heal me so I can do your will and bring you glory.

Shield my life from deadly diseases.

Send your word and heal my diseases.

Let your mercy bring restoration to my soul.

Let your power bring healing to my body.

Protect my bones and make them strong.

Heal my emotions and make me strong.

Restore my health to a vigorous life.

Your Pardon Is Invaluable

Praise the LORD, my soul, and forget not all his benefits – who forgives all your sins and heals all your diseases...

Psalm 103:2-3

He sent out his word and healed them; he rescued them from the grave.

Psalm 107:20

Let your presence bring health and nourishment to my body.

Let my heart be glad and my tongue rejoice.

Give me life and length of days.

You are the Sun of Righteousness rising with healing in its rays.

You are my HEALER!

Father You Comfort Me By Your Spirit

I Seek Your Comfort

Your Comfort Is Uplifting

The LORD Almighty says in Isaiah 51:12

"I, even I, am he who comforts you. Who are you that you fear mere mortals, human beings who are but grass."

You hear my weeping and notice my tears.

Your Holy Spirit is my comforter.

Your Shepherd's rod and staff are my comfort.

Your goodness and kindness are my comfort.

Your tender mercies are my comfort.

Your unfailing love is my comfort.

Your word brings me comfort and relief.

You comfort me as a mother comforts her child.

Your promises preserve my life.

You comfort me in my painful toil.

You comfort me in my suffering.

You have compassion on me when I am afflicted.

You help me with loss and disappointment.

You comfort me when my heart faints within me.

You console me when I am stricken with grief.

You see my cares and take it into your hand.

Your Compassion Is Unfailing

Shout for joy, you heavens; rejoice, you earth; burst into song, you mountains! For the LORD **comforts** his people and will have compassion on his afflicted ones.

Isaiah 49:13

A bruised reed he will not break, and a smoldering wick he will not snuff out. In faithfulness he will bring forth justice;

Isaiah 42:3

You sympathize with me in my weakness.

You don't ever give up on me.

You would not let my hope perish.

Your lovingkindness is more than life to me.

Hear my voice in the morning.

Hold me by your powerful hand.

Lift me up and help me stand.

Relieve me from my anxieties.

Remember me because of your great love.

Remove my sorrow and sighing.

Replace the heaviness in my heart with your praise.

Answer my prayers in your faithfulness.

Surround me with your favor.

Fill my soul with joy and gladness.

Your mercies bring me comfort every morning.

Your comfort births thanksgiving in my heart.

Your Kindness Is Consoling

The LORD, the LORD, the compassionate and gracious God, slow to anger, abounding in love and faithfulness.

Exodus 34:6

You gave me life and showed me kindness, and in your providence watched over my spirit.

Job 10:12

You trade beauty for my brokenness.

You turn my mourning into dancing.

You work out all things for my good.

Your comfort puts songs on my lips.

You are the God of all comfort.

You are the Father of compassion.

You are my COMFORTER!

And forgive us our debts, as we also have forgiven our debtors

Matthew 6:13

SECTION 4

PARDON

Jesus You Have Given Me Your Righteousness

I Seek Your Forgiveness

Jesus Your Precious Blood Purifies Me

But if we walk in the light, as he is in the light, we have fellowship with one another, and the blood of Jesus, his Son, purifies us from all sins.

I John 1:7

The fruit of that righteousness will be peace; its effect will be quietness and confidence forever.

Isaiah 32:17

Forgive my sins and any bad intention of my heart.

Forgive my hidden faults.

Pardon my offenses.

Incline my heart to walk obediently to your word.

Give me the strength to withstand the desires of the flesh.

Purify my heart and make me holy.

Guard the precious truth of the gospel in me.

Help me overcome temptations.

Help me put off the sinful nature.

Help me be truthful.

Help me to live wisely.

Help me know you better every day.

Shine the light of your truth in me.

Help me recall the Word planted in my heart.

Build me up to reflect your kindness.

Put the fear of God in my heart.

Your Righteousness Brings Peace And Joy

Whoever pursues righteousness and love finds life, prosperity and honor.

Proverbs 21:21

Finally, brothers and sisters, whatever is true, whatever is noble, whatever is right, whatever is pure, whatever is lovely, whatever is admirable—if anything is excellent or praiseworthy—think about such things.

Philippians 4:8

Fill my heart with your presence.

Teach me your truth.

Let your word flourish in my heart.

Let the words of my mouth bring you glory.

Let my thoughts be acceptable to You.

Let your righteousness reign in my life.

Let the fruit of righteousness manifest in my life.

I rejoice in your salvation.

I delight to revere your name.

I want a rich and unceasing fellowship with You.

Keep my spirit, soul, and body blameless until the day you come again.

You are my Righteousness!

I Choose To Forgive

A true mark of God's righteousness in our life is forgiving people who hurt us.

A high priest in the Old Testament never sat in the temple or in the tabernacle of worship. We read in Hebrews 8, that Jesus our Great High Priest, having offered himself as a sacrifice on the cross for our sanctification once and for all, entered the true tabernacle of God in heaven with his own precious blood and sat down at the right hand of the Father, His Majesty.

However, as Stephen was stoned to death for witnessing about Jesus as the Messiah, we read, in Acts 7:56b, "I see heaven open and the Son of Man standing at the right hand of God.", and in Acts 7:60, "Lord do not hold this sin against them."

I can only imagine from these verses that when Stephen fell dead, cast off his earthly robe (his mortal body), and entered the courts of heaven, Jesus stood up to honor and receive Stephen's spirit. I think it is because, in Stephen, Jesus saw himself on the cross crying out while in agony, "Father forgive them for they do not know what they are doing" (Luke 24:47). Jesus saw his imprint on Stephen who as he was dying forgave those who were stoning him to death.

We are more like Jesus when we forgive those who hurt us.

Help Me Forgive

Forgive, and you will be forgiven.

Luke 6:37b

But if you do not forgive others their sins, your Father will not forgive your sins.

Matthew 6:15

And when you stand praying, if you hold anything against anyone, forgive them, so that your Father in heaven may forgive you your sins.

Mark 11:25

Lord help me forgive.

Lord I forgive my father _____.

Lord I forgive my mother _____.

Lord I forgive my husband _____.

Lord I forgive my wife _____.

Lord I forgive my brother _____.

Lord I forgive my sister _____.

Lord I forgive my uncle _____.

Lord I forgive my aunt _____.

Lord I forgive my son _____.

Lord I forgive my daughter _____.

Lord I forgive my grandson _____.

Lord I forgive my granddaughter _____.

Lord I forgive my grandfather _____.

Lord I forgive my grandmother _____.

Lord I forgive my cousin _____.

Prayer Notes

Lord I forgive my nephew _____.

Lord I forgive my niece _____.

Lord I forgive my relative _____.

Lord I forgive my school teacher _____.

Lord I forgive my friend _____.

Lord I forgive my coworker _____.

Lord I forgive my neighbor _____.

Lord I forgive my brother in Christ _____.

Lord I forgive my sister in Christ _____.

Lord I forgive my leader _____.

Lord I forgive my mentor _____.

Lord I forgive everyone who has hurt me in the past.

For if you forgive other people when they sin against you,
your heavenly Father will also forgive you.
Matthew 6:14

And lead us not
into temptation
but deliver us
from the evil one

Matthew 6:13

SECTION 5

POWER

Holy Spirit
You Guide
Me By
Your Counsel

I Seek Your Guidance

Your Instruction Is Trustworthy

He guides the humble in what is right and teaches them his way.

Psalm 25:9

I will instruct you and teach you in the way you should go; I will guide you with My eye.

Psalm 32:8
New King James Version (NKJV)

Guide me by your Holy Spirit.

Guide me by your mighty hand.

Lead me in the paths of righteousness.

Instruct me in the way I should go.

Lead me in the way everlasting.

Guide me along the path of peace.

Help me keep moving forward.

Make level the rough ways.

Guide me along the right path.

Lead me in a straight path.

Guide me by your Word.

Your Word is a lamp that lights my way.

Your Word is a light that informs my decisions.

Your Word is living and is actively teaching me.

Your Word judges my thoughts and attitudes.

Your Word rebukes and corrects me.

Your Path Is Right

He refreshes my soul. He guides me along the right paths for his name's sake.

Psalm 23:3

But when he, the Spirit of truth, comes, he will guide you into all the truth. He will not speak on his own; he will speak only what he hears, and he will tell you what is yet to come.

John 16:13

You guide me when I humble myself.

Guide me in your truth.

Write your laws on my heart.

Put your laws in my mind.

Renew my mind in the knowledge of my Creator.

Turn the darkness in my path into light.

Guide me away from the influences that would mislead me.

Direct my heart to your goodness, mercy, and love.

Guide me along the unversed path.

Guide me so my work would not be in vain.

Guide me to friends who love and serve you.

Bring godly mentors along my path.

Help me see the possibilities that are not obvious.

Order my steps to conform to your will.

Guide me according to the plan you have for my life.

Lead me to the springs of living water.

Your Guidance Is Enduring

For this God is our God for ever and ever; he will be our guide even to the end.

Psalm 48:14

Guide me because of your great name.

Guide me by your counsel.

Guide me by your wisdom.

Guide me to your desired outcome.

You will guide me unto the end.

You are my GUIDE!

I Will Rest In The Shadow Of The Almighty

I Seek Your Protection

Your Shelter Is Secure

He will cover you with his feathers, and under his wings you will find refuge; his faithfulness will be your shield and rampart.

Psalm 91:4

But the Lord is faithful, and he will strengthen you and protect you from the evil one.

2 Thessalonians 3:3

You are a shield around me.

You are the stronghold of my life.

You are greater than the one in the world.

Protect my life.

Watch over me.

Protect me from harm.

Protect me from people with bad intentions.

Preserve me from the dread of the enemy.

Guard my steps from the trap of the evil one.

Shield me from the arrows of the evil one.

Raise up a standard against the enemy that seeks to destroy me.

Make the enemy turn back.

Protect me from ways devised to trip me.

Protect me from the lash of the tongue.

Protect me from those who malign me.

You know the anxious thoughts of my heart.

Your Mercy Is Unending

Jesus' prayer in John 17:11, 17:15

I will remain in the world no longer, but they are still in the world, and I am coming to you. Holy Father, **protect** them by the power of your name, the name you gave me, so that they may be one as we are one.

My prayer is not that you take them out of the world but that you **protect** them from the evil one.

Keep me safe from the hands of the wicked.

Protect me for I call on your name.

Give me wisdom that preserves me.

Give me discretion that protects me.

Give me understanding that guards me.

Hold me by your hand and defend me.

Hide me under the shadow of your wings.

Shelter me by your presence.

Guard my course.

Bless my going out and coming in.

Help me dwell in safety.

Keep me as the apple of your eye.

Give your angels to guard me.

Place a hedge of protection around me.

Guard my heart and soul.

Your eyes are always on me.

Your Protection Is Sure

You are my hiding place; you will protect me from trouble and surround me with songs of deliverance.

Psalm 32:7

"Because he loves me," says the Lord, "I will rescue him; I will protect him, for he acknowledges my name."

Psalm 91:14

Your love and faithfulness protect me.

You are my guardian-redeemer.

You are my rear guard.

You are my hiding place.

You are my PROTECTOR!

I Seek Your Deliverance

It is because of God's protection that the devil is unable to snuff the life out of us. The devil has no authority over our lives when we are surrendered to God and are under God's Sovereign rule.

God cannot be tempted with evil nor does He tempt anyone with evil. There is no evil in God. The devil however influences our thoughts and imaginations, and tempts us continuously. When we fall into temptation we give a foothold to the evil one.

In 1 Peter 5:8 we read,

> *"Be alert and of sober mind.*
> *Your enemy the devil prowls around like a roaring lion*
> *looking for someone to devour."*

The devil is throwing his arrows to attack us, spreading his snare to trap us, and hunting us down to rob us of our destiny and to mar the image of God in us. But God who is in us is greater than the evil one in the world. God is faithful to come to our rescue and deliver us from the evil one. All we need to do is to call on Him.

He is our rescue!

Your Deliverance Is Astounding

He got up, rebuked the wind and said to the waves, "Quiet! Be still!" Then the wind died down and it was completely calm.

Mark 4:39

When they came to Jesus, they saw the man who had been possessed by the legion of demons, sitting there, dressed and in his right mind; and they were afraid.

Mark 5:15

Hear my cry for help.

Come to my rescue quickly.

Hear my cry for mercy.

Lift me out of the depths.

Deliver me from depression.

Deliver me from despondency.

Deliver me from my suffering.

Save me out of all my troubles.

Let me not be put to shame.

Free me from my distress.

Destroy the chains that bind me.

Give me relief from my misery.

Destroy the yoke of burden over me.

Defend me against the evil one.

Calm the storm in my life.

Set me free from fear and doubt.

Your Might Is Boundless

Jesus speaking of himself says in Luke 4:18

The Spirit of the Lord is on me, because he has anointed me to proclaim good news to the poor. He has sent me to proclaim freedom for the prisoners and recovery of sight for the blind, to set the oppressed free.

Deliver me from the power of the evil one.

Help me destroy the strongholds in my thoughts and imaginations.

Break the power of addiction over me.

Help me escape the trickery of the enemy.

Foil the plans of the enemy against me.

Hinder the strategies of the enemy against me.

Alert me of the deception of the enemy.

Expose the lies the enemy puts in my mind.

Do not let the will of the enemy prevail against me.

Do not let the enemy triumph over me.

Spare me from going down into the pit.

Deliver me from the hands of evil doers.

Deliver me from the deceitful and the unjust.

Deliver me from abuse and insults.

Bring about justice as I call out to you.

Deliver me to serve you.

Your Power Is Unrestrained

The Lord, the God of battle, has spoken –
who can change his plans? When his hand
moves, who can stop him?

Isaiah 14:27 Living Bible (TLB)

Act on my behalf for I wait on You.

Rescue me from the hand of my oppressors.

Do not turn me over to the desire of my foes.

Shut the mouth of the lions for me.

Uphold my right and my cause.

Vindicate me by your power.

Let no weapon formed against me prosper.

Cause authorities to show me favor.

Cause leaders to have compassion on me.

Deliver me by your powerful hand.

Deliver me because of your compassion.

Delight me with your deliverance.

Surround me with songs of joy.

You are the horn of my salvation.

You are the savior of the world.

You are the deliverer of the needy.

Your Strength Is Awesome

From the Lord comes deliverance. May your blessing be on your people.

Psalm 3:8

You are the rescuer of the weak.

Your strength is awesome.

Your Name is Great.

Your Hand is Mighty.

Your arms are outstretched.

You are my DELIVERER!

Father God Is My Mighty Fortress

I Seek Your Refuge

Your Power Demolish Strongholds

The weapons we fight with are not the weapons of the world. On the contrary, they have divine power to demolish strongholds.

2 Corinthians 6:7

God allows trials in our lives to test our faith in Him, our commitment to Him, and to purify us like a goldsmith refines gold. But we can run into His Everlasting arms, find refuge, and receive strength to endure the trial. God will provide a way for us to keep standing on our feet during the trial and will lead us out of it with greater power than ever before. We read in 1 Corinthians 10:13,

> *"No temptation has overtaken you except what is common to mankind. And God is faithful; he will not let you be tempted beyond what you can bear. But when you are tempted, he will also provide a way out so that you can endure it."*

Trials and testing can come as afflictions or temptations from the devil. For the righteous man, Job, it was affliction. For the Righteous One, Jesus, it was temptation. Jesus was led by the Spirit into the wilderness to be tempted by the devil only to return with more power to minister. When we go through a time of trial and testing, our recourse is to put on the full armor of God and fight the good fight of faith. When the evil one attacks us, we can take refuge in God our mighty fortress. The purpose behind trial and testing is to develop the image of Jesus in us. God is committed to helping us be victorious.

Let us continue to express our trust in Him and rely on His goodness and infinite love.

Your Armor Is Mighty

Put on the full armor of God, so that you can take a stand against the devil's schemes. For our struggle is not against flesh and blood, but against the rulers, against the authorities, against the powers of this dark world and against spiritual forces of evil in the heavenly realms. Therefore put on the full armor of God, so that when the day of evil comes, you may be able to stand your ground, and after you have done everything, to stand.

Ephesians 6:11-13

You have given me the full armor of God.

Your armor is mighty to pulling down strongholds of the devil.

You have given me SALVATION as my helmet.

You have given me FATIH as my shield.

You have given me your RIGHTEOUSNESS as my breastplate.

You have given me the TRUTH, as my belt.

You have given me your SPIRIT and your WORD as my sword.

You have given me your GOSPEL as covering for my feet.

Your gospel on my tongue takes me places where I can glorify you.

You have given me the power to extinguish the flaming arrows of the evil one through faith in you.

You have given me the power to overcome the world through faith in you.

Your righteousness protects my heart from evil desires.

Let your Word train me in righteousness and guard my steps.

Let your Holy Spirit guard my mind from the influence of the evil one.

Let your Holy Spirit bring down strongholds in my mind.

Your Refuge
Is Safe

Have mercy on me, my God, have mercy on me, for in you I take refuge. I will take refuge in the shadow of your wings until the disaster has passed.

Psalm 57:1

...who perseveres under trial because, having stood the test, that person will receive the crown of life that the Lord has promised to those who love him.

James 1:12

You are my tower of strength.

You are my strong fortress.

You are my solid rock.

Give me refuge from the adversary.

Help me for I am confounded.

Give me grace that is sufficient to bear this trial.

Give me comfort amid affliction.

Provide me a way of escape.

Alert me of ways that are not constructive.

You refine me as gold.

Cause my faith to mature.

Help me stand firm.

Fill my heart with courage.

Let me bring glory and honor to your Name.

Let the fruit of the Spirit develop in me.

You are my REFUGE!

Prayer Notes

SECTION 6

CONCLUSION

I am Yours

I Surrender

I Surrender

There is a place of peace, power, and purpose
in this world – and it begins with one word,
Surrender.

Joni Lamb, Surrender All
(Colorado: Waterbrook Press, 2011)

I will worship you.

I will adore you.

I will praise you.

I will sing of you.

I will love you.

I will come before you.

I will lift my hands to you.

I will bow down to you.

I will seek your face.

I will listen to you.

I will wait on you.

I will follow you.

I will trust in you.

I will obey you.

I will honor you.

I will serve you.

I Commit

But you, God, see the trouble of the afflicted;
you consider their grief and take it in hand.
The victims commit themselves to you; you
are the helper of the fatherless.

Psalm 10:14

I will cry out to you.

I will pour out my heart to you.

I will incline my ear to you.

I will raise my eyes to you.

I will look to you for help.

I will rely on you.

I will learn more of you.

I will believe in you.

I will tell of your love.

I will proclaim your goodness.

I will speak of your majesty.

I will tell of your mighty works.

I will bring my tithes to your house.

I will worship you with my offerings.

I will kneel in your awesome presence.

I will prostrate before your throne.

I Rejoice

Let us rejoice and be glad and give him glory! For the wedding of the Lamb has come, and his bride has made herself ready.

Revelation 19:7

I will bless you.

I will exalt you.

I will say you are my God.

I will say you are my Father.

I will say you are my Lord.

I will say you are my King.

I will live FOR you today.

I will live WITH you forever!

Amen

"Amen! Praise and glory and wisdom and thanks and honor and power and strength be to our God forever and ever. Amen!"

Revelation 7:12

Now to King eternal, immortal, invisible, the only God, be honor and glory for ever and ever. Amen.

1 Timothy 1:17

Concluding Thought

God so loved the world that he gave his Son Jesus to pay the penalty for our sins. By acknowledging Jesus Christ as our Lord and Savior, and asking him to forgive our sins, we receive the gift of eternal life. Then when we die and our mortal bodies return to the earth from which they were formed, our spirits born again in Christ Jesus will go back to God.

Finally, we will be clothed again with an immortal resurrected body, and live with God forever and ever.

If Jesus is not your Savior and Lord, invite him today to be the Lord of your life. He longs for you to know him.

A Simple Prayer

Lord Jesus, I believe you are the Son of God and you died for me. I ask you to forgive my sins. I receive the gift of eternal life that you have offered through your death on the cross. I thank you for forgiving all my sins.

Father God, I thank you for Jesus Christ. I thank you for the Holy Spirit. Fill me with your Holy Spirit to guide me, and to help me do your will. I want to fulfil your purpose for my life. I ask this in Jesus name.

Amen.

Know that God has a great plan for your life. You are created for his purpose. The Holy Spirit lives inside of you to guide you, and to empower you to do his will. As you obey the promptings of the Holy Spirt, pursue righteousness, faith, love, and peace, you will experience the abundant life Jesus died to give you.

Your best life is ahead!

I pray for God's love and peace to be poured into your heart in great measure as you declare His praises and present your requests with thanksgiving every day.

About the Author

The author grew up in a five-generation missionary family, dedicated to spreading the gospel around the world. She draws on her experience of planting churches, pioneering a Christian school, ministering in songwriting and teaching God's word, raising two now adult children, living in multiple continents, and eventually working in corporate America, to bless others with what she has learned and experienced with the help of the Holy Spirit.

Printed in the United States
By Bookmasters